to:

from:

Published by Sellers Publishing, Inc.

161 John Roberts Road, South Portland, ME 04106
Visit us at www.sellerspublishing.com • E-mail: rsp@rsvp.com

Compiled by Robin Haywood.
Photo Editors: Mary Baldwin, Amanda Mooney

ISBN 13: 978-1-4162-4523-0

Printed and bound in China.
Cover image © 2014 Sabine Rath

10 9 8 7 6 5 4 3 2 1

Cat Naps

the key to contentment

SELLERS

PUBLISHING

Life is hard,
then you nap.

Author unknown

The idea of calm
exists in a sitting cat.

Jules Renard

There is more to life
than increasing its speed.

Mohandas Gandhi

8

If I didn't wake up,
I'd still be sleeping!

Yogi Berra

I don't know why it is we
are in such a hurry to get
up when we fall down. You
might think we would lie
there and rest for a while.

Max Forrester Eastman

If there were to be
a universal sound
depicting peace,
I would surely vote
for the purr.

Barbara L. Diamond

15

Learning to ignore
things is one of the
great paths to
inner peace.

Robert J. Sawyer

How beautiful it is to do nothing,
and then to rest afterward.

Spanish proverb

Champagne wishes
and caviar dreams . . .

Author unknown

Cats are rather delicate creatures and they are subject to a good many ailments, but I never heard of one who suffered from insomnia.

Joseph Wood Krutch

A cat pours his
body on the
floor like water.
It is restful just
to see him.

William Lyon Phelps

I have never taken
any exercise except
sleeping and resting.

Mark Twain (Samuel L. Clemens)

Who among us hasn't envied a cat's ability to ignore the cares of daily life and to relax completely?

Karen Brademeyer

Take rest;
a field that has rested
gives a bountiful crop.

Ovid

O sleep, it is a gentle thing,
Belov'd from pole to pole!

Samuel Taylor Coleridge

Sleep is the
best meditation.

Tenzin Gyatso,
the 14th Dalai Lama

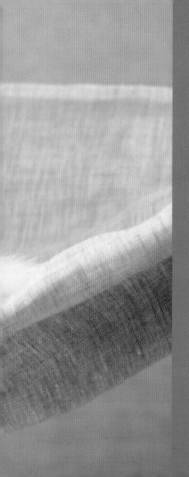

There's never enough
time to do all the
nothing you want.

Bill Watterson,
"Calvin and Hobbes"

Loafing needs no explanation
and is its own excuse.

Christopher Morley

Yawn and the world
yawns with you.
Snore and you
sleep alone.

Author unknown

Nature does not
hurry, yet everything
is accomplished.

Lao Tzu

No day is so bad it can't
be fixed with a nap.

Carrie Snow

Very little is needed
to make a happy life . . .

Marcus Aurelius Antoninus

If there is one spot
of sun spilling onto
the floor, a cat will
find it and soak it up.

Jean Asper McIntosh

It takes a lot of time to be a genius. You have to sit around so much doing nothing, really doing nothing.

Gertrude Stein

Slow down and everything you are chasing will come around and catch you.

John DePaola

The fog comes
on little cat feet.

Carl Sandburg,
"The Fog"

Follow your bliss
and the universe
will open doors for
you where there
were only walls.

Joseph Campbell

Kittens are born with their eyes shut. They open them in about six days, take a look around, then close them again for the better part of their lives.

Stephen Baker

Everything I know
I learned from my cat:
When you're hungry, eat.
When you're tired,
nap in a sunbeam.
When you go to the vet's,
pee on your owner.

Gary Smith

Don't underestimate
the value of Doing Nothing,
of just going along,
listening to all the things
you can't hear,
and not bothering.

A. A. Milne,
Pooh's Little Instruction Book

Credits